everyone's-a-winner games for children's ministry

Group

Loveland, Colorado

everyone's-a-winner games for children's ministry
Copyright © 1995 Group Publishing, Inc.

Credits
Contributing Authors: Michelle Anthony, Lorie W. Barnes, Jody Brolsma, Jacqui Dunham, Nanette Goings, Susan Grover, Steven Henkel, Jan Kershner, Dan McGill, Pam Montgomery, Lori Haynes Niles, Mary Van Aalsburg, and Carla Williams
Book Acquisitions Editors: Mike Nappa and Susan L. Lingo
Editor: Liz Shockey
Creative Products Director: Joani Schultz
Copy Editor: Amy Simpson
Art Director and Designer: Lisa Chandler
Cover Art Director: Liz Howe
Computer Graphic Artist: Kari Monson
Cover Illustrator: Neecy Twinem
Illustrator: Rebecca McKillip Thornburgh
Production Manager: Gingar Kunkel

Unless otherwise noted, Scriptures quoted from The Youth Bible, New Century Version, copyright © 1991 by Word Publishing, Dallas, Texas 75039. Used by permission.

Library of Congress Cataloging-in-Publication Data
Everyone's-a-winner : games for children's ministry.
        p.   cm.
     ISBN 1-55945-697-3
     1. Church work with children. 2. Activity programs in Christian education. 3. Games.
     BV639.C4E94 1995
     259'.22–dc20   95-23215
                                                               CIP
10 9 8 7 6 5 4 3 2   04 03 02 01 00 99 98 97 96
Printed in the United States of America.

coNteNts

coNteNts

contents

OUTDOOR GAMES

contents

iNtroductioN

Kids need to play. Many child-development experts claim that children need the release and the increased confidence that games offer. But games in many books actually do the opposite—they undermine kids' confidence levels, pressuring them to "be the fastest," "jump the highest," and "win, win, win!" When we place children in win-lose games and activities, no one wins.

The games included in Group's *Everyone's-a-Winner Games for Children's Ministry* are radically different from those found in other game books. Group Publishing's authors and editors have collected and field-tested over 100 exciting games and activities that are cooperative, not competitive. These games affirm children and help build community, not tear it down. Everyone has fun, everyone experiences success, and everyone wins!

Included in Group's *Everyone's-a-Winner Games for Children's Ministry* are exciting games, races, relays, and other activities for elementary-age kids. There are classroom games, gymnasium games, games for the great outdoors, and even games to play while you're traveling. And the handy index at the back of the book allows you to choose games according to their energy levels so no matter where you are or what you're doing, you'll have just the right game or activity for your kids.

Enjoy these games and provide "no-fail fun" for the children in your ministry.

classroom games

An Introduction to Classroom Games

Kids often view their classroom as a boring, ordinary place. But these games will shake up ordinary classroom days and make inside playtimes on even the rainiest days extraordinarily fun! A game a day keeps your kids healthy and happy and looking forward to classroom times.

Be sure to clear open spaces in which to safely play games, or select games that require low energy levels. If rules call for running, substitute jogging, walking backward, or crawling. On a rainy day, try inviting another group of kids into your room for "tame-game time" and playing a variety of low-energy classroom games together!

danglin' donuts

Best For: Kindergarten through sixth grade
Energy Level: Medium
Supplies: Donuts, string, scissors, newspapers, a timer or watch with a second hand, and cups of chilled apple cider

THE GAME:

Danglin' Donuts is especially fun to play in the fall or winter when it's followed by chilled apple cider.

Before the game, cut a 24-inch piece of string for each child. Tie a donut on one end of each string.

Invite kids to form pairs and decide who will be the first "donut dangler" and who will be the first "donut chaser." Hand each pair a sheet of newspaper (crumb catcher) and two donuts on strings. Direct the donut chasers to kneel on the newspapers with their hands clasped behind their backs. Have the donut danglers dangle a donut in front of each chaser. Encourage the donut chasers to gobble as much of their donuts as possible in one minute. If donuts fall off the strings, have partners set their donuts aside and wait until you call time. At the end of one minute, have partners switch roles then dangle and eat the other donuts.

When you're finished with the game, let kids finish their donuts and enjoy chilled apple cider.

lots of laughs

Best For: All ages
Energy Level: Low
Supplies: At least one inflated balloon

THE GAME:

This game is sure to tickle your fancy and is a great icebreaker at parties. Have children sit in a circle. Tell kids that when you toss the inflated balloon into the air, everyone has to laugh—and keep laughing—while the balloon is airborne. As soon as the balloon touches the ground, everyone must stop laughing. Anyone caught giggling after the balloon touches the ground must hop around the circle once. As the game progresses, you will be tickled to see how much harder it becomes to stop laughing on cue.

For "group giggles," form small groups of three or four kids and hand each group a balloon. Have them play just as if they were a large group.

This game is especially fun at parties, retreats, and overnighters!

wrap-o-rama

Best For: All ages
Energy Level: Medium
Supplies: Sheets of paper, crayons, rubber bands, cereal boxes, squares of gift wrap, and tape

THE GAME:

This great group activity builds cooperation, communication, and affirmation skills in a humorous way.

Form trios and give each trio three rubber bands, a square of gift wrap, tape, three sheets of paper, and crayons.

Have trio members link their wrists together with rubber bands so that each member is connected to the other two members in the threesome. Challenge kids to use their paper and crayons to create three colorful pictures that show ways friends help each other, such as mowing the grass, washing dishes, or picking up toys. Then instruct kids to put the finished pictures in the cereal boxes and to gift-wrap the boxes. Assure kids that artistic ability isn't important—creative cooperation is the goal!

After you're finished wrapping, have trios pass their gifts to other groups. Be sure each group has three gifts to open, then unwrap the gifts and tape the drawings to the wall to remind kids that it is fun to work together.

t.p. tangle

Best For: All ages
Energy Level: Medium
Supplies: Several rolls of toilet paper

THE GAME:

This game ties up your kids in a tangle of fun!

Have kids stand in a line, all facing the same way. Give the first person in line a roll of toilet paper ("T.P."). Instruct the first person to step on the tissue then carefully pass the roll through his or her legs to the next person in line. Direct that person to pass the T.P. roll over his or her shoulder to the next person. Have the kids continue to pass the tissue over and under until it reaches the end of the line. Then have them pass the roll back up to the front of the line in the same way. If the toilet paper breaks at any time, have them start over. Can they do a whole roll? It takes lots of cooperation!

You may wish to use yarn or string if you're concerned about using too much bathroom tissue. When you're finished, see if kids can reverse the process by winding the yarn back into a ball!

rumble and reverse

Best For: Second through sixth grade
Energy Level: Medium
Supplies: Chairs

THE GAME:

This active game is a blast! It gets its name from the sounds the chairs make.

Place chairs in a close circle, facing the center. Have enough chairs for everyone minus one. Choose one child to be the "chair snatcher" and to stand in the center of the circle. Have the rest of the group sit in the chairs.

When the chair snatcher yells "Rumble," begin the game. Players move one chair to the right while the chair snatcher tries to find a seat to sit in. Movement continues to the right until the chair snatcher says "reverse." Then everyone moves to the left. The chair snatcher may call "reverse" at any time. When the chair snatcher finally snatches a seat, the person to his or her left becomes the new chair snatcher.

For added excitement with older kids, choose two or three players to be chair snatchers.

the cotton bowl

Best For: Kindergarten through second grade
Energy Level: Medium
Supplies: Cotton balls, plastic spoons, bowls, blindfolds, and
                   a watch with a second hand

THE GAME:

Form groups of up to six players and have each group sit in a circle. Let each group choose one player to be "It." Blindfold each It and have him or her sit with a plastic spoon and a bowl in the center of the group's circle. Scatter cotton balls inside each circle.

On "go," have the blindfolded players use their spoons to scoop up cotton balls and put them in their bowls. Encourage the rest of the players in each group to use "hot" or "cold" clapping to help It locate the cotton balls. Have kids clap fast when It is close to a cotton ball and clap more slowly if It moves away from cotton balls. At the end of 30 seconds, call a timeout and count the number of cotton balls in each bowl. Then let each group blindfold a new person and play again.

Save the cotton balls to use later in craft projects. (They make great lambs for a lesson on the Good Shepherd!)

. . . .

who am i?

Best For: First through sixth grade
Energy Level: Medium
Supplies: 3x5 cards, tape, and a marker

THE GAME:

This is a super icebreaker for parties or for the beginning of a new year.
Before this game, draw pictures on 3x5 cards. Draw simple pictures such as Bible characters, foods, or animals. You may wish to choose characters or objects that correspond to your lesson topics.

As kids arrive, tape a card to each child's forehead without letting the children see the pictures or words.

Then challenge the kids to ask each other questions to discover who or what they are. Encourage kids to ask questions such as "Am I a person?" "Am I a guy or a girl?" "What did I do in the Bible?"

Allow kids to circulate and ask questions for five minutes. Then let kids tell who or what they are. If some are still unsure, offer clues to help them guess.

Here are some suggestions for characters and objects to use on the cards, but the possibilities are endless.

animals	bible characters	foods
● zebra	● Moses with the Ten Commandments	● taco
● kangaroo	● Joshua at the wall of Jericho	● chicken wing
● monkey	● Noah with the ark	● pizza
	● Joseph with his colored coat	

zoo who?

Best For: Second through sixth grade
Energy Level: Low
Supplies: Modeling dough, 3×5 cards, pencils, and a plastic bowl

THE GAME:

Give your kids a chance to use their creativity in this game that ends up being a real zoo!

Form two groups and have them sit across from each other. Hand each child a 3×5 card and a pencil. Have each child draw an animal on his or her card then drop the card into a plastic bowl.

Give each child a lump of mod-

> **Modeling Dough**
>
> Heat 1½ cups water and ½ cup salt almost to boiling. Remove from heat and stir in 2 tablespoons vegetable oil, 2 tablespoons alum, and food coloring if desired. Cool the mixture, then knead until it's smooth. Store dough in an airtight bag.

eling dough. Let someone from one group draw an animal card from the bowl and secretly show the card to the other members of his or her group. Then have everyone in the group make that animal from modeling dough while the other group guesses what animal is being formed. The children making the animals are allowed to give sound clues such as barking, mooing, or roaring. Play until each dough animal has been identified.

chalkboard charlie

Best For: Kindergarten through third grade
Energy Level: Medium
Supplies: Chalk and a chalkboard

THE GAME:

Use this game as a fun way to spark quick thinking and originality within your group. This game is also a perfect springboard for a discussion about the unique qualities of individuals.

Before this activity, draw a large outline of a person on each side of the chalkboard. Make sure there is chalk beneath each drawing. If you don't have a chalkboard, tape two large sheets of white shelf paper to the wall and use markers. If the weather is nice, play outside and use washable sidewalk chalk.

Have children form two lines facing the chalkboard, at the opposite end of the room. Direct the first child in each line to hop to the chalkboard and draw one feature on the figure, such as an eye, an arm, or an ear. Then have the child hop back and hand the chalk to the next child in line. Have children continue playing until each one has had a turn to add a feature to the figure.

If young children have trouble thinking of features to add, suggest such details as eyes, ears, teeth, fingers, shoes, buttons, and jewelry. When the game is over, compare your chalkboard people.

For extra fun, try to create personalities for the figures: Give them names and guess what they do for a living.

balloon bop

Best For: First through sixth grade
Energy Level: Medium
Supplies: 10- to 12-inch balloons

THE GAME:

You'll need one or two inflated and tied 10- to 12-inch balloons for the game, but have extras ready in case of blowouts.

Have children stand in a small circle and face one another. Explain that children will hit the balloon to each other using different parts of their bodies. While they are playing, have the group sing a song such as "Heads, Shoulders, Knees, and Toes." Start the song and show kids how to use their heads, shoulders, knees, and toes to hit the balloon. Sing slowly at first, then speed up as kids get the hang of it. See how long you can keep the hoppin' and boppin' going before your balloon touches the ground.

Have older kids call out ways to bop the balloon, such as with their wrists, ankles, elbows, or noses. Eventually begin adding balloons to see how many you can keep boppin' at one time.

putt-putt

Best For: All ages
Energy Level: Low
Supplies: None

THE GAME:

Kids love this "drive-'em-crazy" game.

Have kids sit in a circle on the floor. Choose one player to be the "key person." Have everyone hold an imaginary steering wheel. The key person starts the game by saying, "Putt-putt, putt-putt." Then the key person "signals" a right turn by tapping the person on his or her right. That person quickly says "putt-putt" and taps the next player. Continue around the circle until someone calls out "screech!" Players hold their steering wheels straight and lean back as though they're applying the brakes on their pretend cars. Play switches direction and the car is in reverse. Tell kids they may each call out "screech" only once during the game.

The fun of Putt-Putt is in speedy response time.

For a real challenge with advanced players, start two cars going in opposite directions—and watch out for funny "collisions!"

block lock

Best For: All ages
Energy Level: Medium
Supplies: 40 building blocks, a marker, masking tape, and a paper grocery sack

THE GAME:

This game is guaranteed to "build" group unity.

You'll need 40 building blocks for this game. Apply a piece of masking tape to each block, then number pairs of blocks from one to 20. Place the blocks in the paper grocery sack.

Distribute the blocks to the kids. Tell kids that the object of this game is to see how fast the group can build a skyscraper. But before they can build, they have to match the numbers on their blocks. Say "go" and encourage kids to call out the numbers on their blocks to find matching pairs. You may wish to begin with number one and work your way up from there. Have pairs put their blocks together and work with other pairs to combine the blocks into a building. Suggest building one building straight up and in the next round building horizontally.

Have older children dismantle the skyscraper in reverse numerical order.

calculator kids

Best For: Second through sixth grade
Energy Level: Medium
Supplies: 3x5 cards, a marker, and tape

THE GAME:

Anyway you add it up, Calculator Kids brings a group together.

Before the game, write the numbers from zero to 15 on 3x5 cards, one number per card.

Give each child a numbered card to tape to the front of his or her shirt. Some children may have more than one number card, depending on the size of your group. Have an adult leader call out a number "answer." As an answer is given, direct kids to form groups of numbers that equal that number. For example, if the leader says "six," kids with the numbers four and two or five and one can form groups.

Continue calling numbers to form different number combinations. As kids get the idea, go faster! For the final round, use the total sum of the group's numbers as the answer you call, and form a giant mathematical hug.

For a snappy variation with older kids, use subtraction. If three is called, then 10 and seven or nine and six or four and one can link up.

ha! hee! ho!

Best For: Kindergarten through third grade
Energy Level: Low
Supplies: None

THE GAME:

This is a good icebreaker for a party or a first-of-the-year event.
Number off by saying "ha," "hee," and "ho" instead of "one," "two,"
and "three." Mix the group by having the kids close their eyes and turn
three circles in place. Explain to the kids that when you say "go," each one
may find his or her group by saying the special word, "ha," "hee," or "ho."
Once one group member locates another, have the two join hands and
find the rest of their group.

When all the group members have been found, challenge each group to
say their laughter word, "ha," "hee," or "ho," 10 times with straight faces.
Allow the other groups to make silly faces to get them to laugh. If a group
can keep straight faces, let them line up first for drinks of water.

ballooNegories

Best For: First through sixth grade
Energy Level: Medium
Supplies: One or two 10- to 12-inch balloons

THE GAME:

This game brings lots of smiles and laughter. Be prepared for some crazy
answers!

Form two groups. Instruct groups to stand facing one another. Have
children hit a 10- to 12-inch balloon back and forth between groups.
Encourage kids to make the balloon go high when they bop it. Let kids
enjoy bopping the balloons for a few minutes. Then have an adult leader
call out a category such as foods, cereals, names of boys or girls, or makes
of cars. Each player can say the name of an item from that category when
he or she bops the balloon. For instance, if the category is fruit, the first
player to bop the balloon might say "orange." The next player might say
"grape." Continue bopping the balloon and naming items until kids can
name no more without repeating some.

Determine categories based on age. For younger children, try

- fruit,
- animals,
- sports, and
- colors.

For older children, try
- pizza toppings,
- sea animals,
- board games, and
- musical instruments.

For an additional challenge with older kids, play with two balloons in each group. You'll be surprised at how funny some of the answers will be after kids have covered a few categories.

tickly winks

Best For: Kindergarten through fourth grade
Energy Level: Low
Supplies: Chairs

THE GAME:

This game calls for lots of giggles and laughter; make sure you have plenty on hand!

Place enough chairs in a circle so that half of your group can sit down.

Form two equal groups. Have one group sit in the chairs with their backs touching the backs of the chairs. They are the Movers. Have the rest of the kids each choose a chair to stand behind. They are the Ticklers.

The leader walks around the outside of the chairs while the Movers watch the leader. Ticklers keep their heads down. The leader winks at one of the Movers. That player tries to stand up without getting tickled by the Tickler behind his or her chair. If the Mover is tickled, he or she switches places with the Tickler. If not, the game continues. After three rounds, have Movers and Ticklers switch places and roles.

For more fun, have the leader wink at more than one player at a time. Make sure the leader doesn't get something in his or her eye, or you'll have everybody jumping.

clappy cat

Best For: Kindergarten through third grade
Energy Level: Medium
Supplies: None

THE GAME:

In this cat-and-mouse game, the mice come to the cat.

Have players form a circle. Choose one player to be the "sleeping cat." The cat stands in the center of the circle with eyes closed and hands about one foot apart, ready to clap. Have the other children act like mice and creep around the cat, making quiet, mousey squeaks. Tell the mice to try to tap the palm of one of the cat's "paws."

If the cat feels a mouse, the cat claps his or her paws before the mouse escapes. If any part of the mouse's paw is touched, the mouse becomes the cat and the cat goes to the center of the circle for a "catnap." When only one mouse remains in the circle, he or she becomes the first cat for the next game.

secret shake

Best For: Third through sixth grade
Energy Level: Medium
Supplies: Blindfolds if necessary

THE GAME:

This game is especially fun when you play it in a totally dark room or outside at night. If your room isn't dark, use blindfolds or have kids close their eyes instead. Make sure to clear enough space for safety.

Have children choose partners. Encourage pairs to find places in the room to meet. Allow the pairs two minutes to create secret handshakes. Challenge them to use combinations of several motions. Demonstrate an example before the group (with the help of another adult leader), using the following sequence of actions:

- a high-five (partners slap hands high in the air),
- a double pump (a standard handshake twice),
- the clasp (partners clasp hands), and
- a single pump (one standard handshake).

After pairs have developed their secret handshakes, bring the group together and ask everyone to scatter. Then turn off the lights, put on blindfolds, or have the kids close their eyes. Instruct kids to locate their partners by using their secret handshakes. They'll have fun shaking others' hands before they find their partners. When pairs match up, have them stand still until everyone has found his or her partner.

Have kids congratulate each other with nice, firm handshakes and gentle pats on the back.

· ·

just bead it!

Best For: First through sixth grade
Energy Level: Medium
Supplies: Large craft beads, string or yarn, tape, a large bowl, and a table

THE GAME:

Before this game, make four necklaces, using large craft beads. Make each necklace with at least six beads, using a different color pattern for each one. For example, use a red-red-blue-yellow-green-green pattern for one strand and a blue-red-blue-red-yellow-red-yellow-red pattern for another. Cut four 16-inch lengths of string or yarn.

Place a large bowl of colorful craft beads on a table in the center of the room. Securely tape one end of a string to each side of the table. Tape a sample necklace beside each string. Set extra tape on the table.

Form four groups and have them line up, each in a different corner of the room. On "go," have the first person in each line hop to the table and

look at the sample bead pattern on his or her necklace. Have the first player in each line string the first bead in the pattern then hop back to the line. The next person then hops forward to string the second bead. Continue until each group finishes the bead pattern. Tie the ends of the strings to make necklaces. After each necklace is complete, tape new pieces of string to the table and have groups switch sides and patterns. Continue stringing beads until there's a necklace for everyone in the group.

Have kids wear their necklaces to show everyone that your group cooperates and works together—and has gobs of fun, too.

five fUNNY faces

Best For: All ages
Energy Level: Low
Supplies: Markers, sheets of paper, tape, and a watch with a second hand

THE GAME:

Kids will love playing this game that makes everyone "look good."
Form groups of five. Tape five sheets of paper to a wall for each group. Tell the kids that they'll be drawing special facial features on each of their groups' papers. Assign each child a facial feature such as a nose, a head, hair, a mouth, eyes, or ears. Have each child stand in front of a paper and draw his or her assigned facial feature with a marker.

Begin the game by saying "go." Every 10 seconds, call out "switch!" then have members go to other pieces of their group's papers and draw.

For example, the "nose" person will draw five noses, one on each sheet of paper for his or her group; the "hair" person will draw five hairstyles on the papers; and so on. Since drawing order will be at random, kids will draw some silly faces!

When all the faces are done, encourage kids to think of names for their wacky characters. Then let kids tell one thing about each character, such as "This is Purple Petunia" or "Silly Sam loves to eat pizza and pickles for breakfast."

jelly beaN swap

Best For: First through sixth grade
Energy Level: Low
Supplies: Sheets of paper, pencils, multicolored jelly beans, plastic sandwich bags, and a clear plastic jar

THE GAME:

This game's a sweet treat to play, but save some of the jelly beans for a yummy treat.

Separate the jelly beans by color into plastic sandwich bags, placing 12 jelly beans (all one color) in each bag. You'll need one bag of jelly beans for every two or three kids; for example, one pair will have green jelly beans, another pair will have red.

Invite kids to form pairs or trios. Give each group a bag of jelly beans, a sheet of paper, and a pencil. Ask each group to write or draw a list of 12 things that are the same color as the jelly beans in its bag.

After groups have their lists ready, instruct one member of each group to hold the list and the other to hold the bag of candy. Direct the groups to take turns guessing objects on each other's lists. Tell groups to exchange one jelly bean every time a correct guess is made. Have them continue taking turns guessing items until each group has at least one of each color of jelly bean.

Empty the "used" jelly beans into a clear plastic jar as a colorful reminder of how your group looks when it's working together. Pass out fresh jelly beans as a special treat to eat.

COMMUNicatioN statioN

Best For: Third through sixth grade
Energy Level: Low
Supplies: Photocopies of the "My Favorite Things" list (p. 27) and pencils

THE GAME:

Before the game, make one photocopy of the "My Favorite Things" list (p. 27) for each child.

Distribute the photocopies and pencils. Ask kids to answer the questions without revealing their answers to each other. When everyone has finished, shuffle the papers and pass them out. Be sure no one receives his or her own paper. Invite kids to ask questions that will help them discover whose papers they have, such as "Who likes pizza and green olives?" or "Who'd like to be a firefighter someday?" Have kids take turns asking questions until they have revealed everyone's identity.

My favorite things

- My favorite food is _____.

- My favorite color is _____.

- I have a _____ for a pet.

- When I grow up, I would like to be _____.

• •

wrap it up!

Best For: Third through sixth grade
Energy Level: Medium
Supplies: Rolls of white toilet paper (four rolls per group), cotton balls, ribbon, stick-on bows, and lunch sacks

THE GAME:

This game reinforces the idea that each of us is a unique gift from God. This game is best played with a few helpers.

Place rolls of white toilet paper, cotton balls, ribbon, and stick-on bows in five lunch sacks.

Form five groups and hand each group a lunch sack. Let each group choose a person to be the "gift." The object of the game is for groups to wrap their gifts, using the tissue, ribbon, cotton balls, and bows—and their imagination!

When groups are done, let them introduce each gift and tell something special about that gift, such as "Our gift likes to help people" or "This gift is friendly to everyone."

Vary this activity to coordinate with the themes of your lessons. For instance, if you're studying about Daniel and the lions' den, give the kids yellow and brown crepe paper and have them wrap up a "ferocious lion." At Christmastime, make snowmen—add hats and scarves to the sacks.

food features

Best For: Kindergarten through third grade
Energy Level: Low
Supplies: None

THE GAME:

This game is great when you have just a little time to fill or when you need to calm the children after a wild activity.

Encourage the children to sit on the floor in a circle. Have them think of things they like to eat. Choose a child to act out each food or to act out eating the food. For example, if they act out gelatin, they can wiggle and shiver, or they can hop up and down to act out popcorn.

If no one guesses what food the child is acting out, he or she may give verbal clues.

For older kids, write some of the foods listed below on slips of paper, then let kids act them out. Some fun foods might include

- bacon frying in a pan,
- pigs in a blanket,
- hot dogs,
- ice cubes in soda pop,
- popcorn,
- scrambled eggs,
- bubble gum, or
- toasting marshmallows.

This game makes everyone hungry, so serve a simple treat like apples when you're done playing.

building bethlehem

Best For: Fourth through sixth grade
Energy Level: Medium
Supplies: Building blocks and boxes of various sizes

THE GAME:

Even if it's not Christmas, this is a great game to help kids remember the story.

Invite kids to form small groups of four to five. Give each group an equal number of building blocks and boxes. Encourage kids to think about the Christmas story and what it must have been like in Bethlehem. Have kids take a few minutes to build things that were in Bethlehem the night Jesus was born, such as a stable, a manger, an inn, animals, or trees.

When everyone finishes building, gather the kids together and have them take turns telling the story of the first Christmas, using what they've made.

farm families

Best For: First through second grade
Energy Level: Medium
Supplies: Popped popcorn, plastic spoons, paper lunch sacks, and cups of juice

THE GAME:

Young children will delight in this game of "gathering grain." In the process, they'll be learning to work together toward a common goal.

Tell children to pretend they're farmers in a field. First they have to plant their seeds. Let each child take a small handful of popped popcorn and sprinkle it around the room. Then have children form two to four farm families. Hand each family a paper lunch sack to place in a corner of the room. Give each child a plastic spoon.

Tell children that when you flip the lights off and on, they'll scoop up their harvest. Instruct children in each family to scoop up popcorn with their spoons then empty the popcorn into their family's sack.

Have kids continue playing until all the popcorn has been "harvested." Let kids compare the amounts of grain they harvested and congratulate each other on a job well done.

Serve fresh popcorn and cups of juice for "family treats." Then put the old popcorn out for squirrels and birds to enjoy.

Matchmakers

Best For: First through sixth grade
Energy Level: Low
Supplies: 3x5 cards and pencils

THE GAME:

This fun twist on the game Concentration helps kids have fun while they learn one another's names. It's a great game for the early part of a year together.

Hand each child two 3x5 cards. Have the children form small groups of five to eight participants. Tell each child to print his or her first name on one card and last name on the other. Instruct younger children to draw matching shapes on their cards to help kids who aren't reading yet.

Collect the cards, keeping each group's cards separate. Have an adult leader shuffle the cards and place them face down in rows of four or five, setting them up like a Memory or Concentration game board. Let children take turns turning over two cards at a time, looking for matches. Any time a child makes a match, he or she gets another turn. When all the cards have been picked up, instruct kids to collect their own name cards, form new groups, and play again.

Once this game is over, kids will know who "that one kid" is and can start using his or her name.

huff 'N' puff

Best For: All ages
Energy Level: Medium
Supplies: Several table tennis balls and masking tape

THE GAME:

This is a great game for fostering team spirit.

Place a line of masking tape on the floor on each side of the room. Form two groups. Have half of each group form a line behind the tape on one side of the room. Direct the other half to form a line facing them behind the other tape. Starting on the same side, give the first child in each line a table tennis ball. On "go," have kids propel their table tennis balls to the tape on the opposite side of the room by blowing. No hands or nose nudges allowed! When a child reaches the tape on the other side of the room, have him or her sit down and let the first child in that line blow the ball back. Play continues until all children are sitting down.

center spot

Best For: All ages
Energy Level: Medium
Supplies: None

THE GAME:

This is a wonderful icebreaker!

Tell kids to sit in a circle and choose one child to be the "center spot." Have the center spot stand in the center of the circle. Encourage kids to "interview" the center spot by asking get-to-know-you questions such as "What's your favorite food?" or "When is your birthday?" After three questions, have everyone say, "We love you; who do you love?" The center spot answers with a statement that involves other kids, such as "I love all people who wear blue tennis shoes!" Then everyone with blue tennis shoes stands up and races to find a new place to sit while the center spot steals a seat. The person without a place to sit becomes the next center spot.

For a real treat, ask someone to videotape the game, then watch it together at your next group get-together.

wet Noodle

Best For: Kindergarten through second grade
Energy Level: Medium
Supplies: Large pieces of cooked spaghetti or lasagna noodles, water, and paper towels

THE GAME:

In this game, no one wants to be stuck with a wet noodle!

Have kids sit in a circle. Dip a spaghetti or lasagna noodle in water, then pass the noodle around the circle. When the leader claps, the child holding the noodle stands up. He or she may dip the noodle in water then pass it along as he or she continues standing. Each time the leader claps, the child holding the noodle stands up and continues passing the noodle. Have kids continue playing until only one child remains sitting in the circle.

This game is especially fun during an evening retreat with a spaghetti supper!

scramble up!

Best For: Fourth through sixth grade
Energy Level: Low
Supplies: 3x5 cards, scissors, and pencils

THE GAME:

Cut 3x5 cards into quarters to make a stack of small paper squares. Have children write their first names on the squares, using one square per letter. Have each child find a partner, then have each pair join another pair to form a game group. Instruct kids to look at their letters and think of words they can spell using those letters. Instruct one pair in each game group to lay down a word. Direct the other pair to form a word to connect with that word. Continue for two minutes with pairs taking turns forming words. Then have kids in each game group switch partners, collect their letters, and form a new game group with another pair. Play a couple more rounds for fun.

To add greater challenge, allow kids to use the letters of their last names, too. For more variation, let everyone work together to make a giant crossword puzzle.

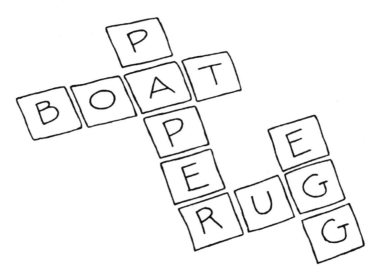

classroom games

gymnasium games

An Introduction to Gymnasium Games

Kids love to move and play in gymnasiums and other big areas. But if your church doesn't have access to a gym, don't panic. Any large, open space will work for these exciting, energetic games. Spacious rooms devoid of furniture and other obstacles attract kids like magnets. There's something inviting about being allowed—even *encouraged*—to run, jump, and hoot and holler inside. Why, that's only supposed to happen outside!

Make the most of large indoor play areas and offer kids a selection of games to play any time—rain or shine.

squeeze play

Best For: Kindergarten through second grade
Energy Level: Medium
Supplies: A plastic hoop

THE GAME:

This is a great icebreaker game guaranteed to generate giggles and grins. Lay a plastic hoop in the center of the play area. If you have more than 20 kids, use two plastic hoops.

Have kids number off by fives, then let them scatter around the edges of the playing area. Choose one child to be the caller and have him or her stand beside the plastic hoop. Tell the caller to shout out a number between 1 and 5. Kids whose number is called must hop to the center of the room and stand inside the plastic hoop. Both feet of each child must be inside the hoop. Encourage kids to make a "squeeze play" if players have trouble fitting inside the hoop. If everyone successfully squeezes into the hoop, have kids return to their places for another round. If someone doesn't fit, he or she (or pairs of kids) becomes the next caller.

Invite the caller to shout out two—or even three—numbers per round. End the game by calling out all the numbers and going for a group squeeze!

For a different twist, let kids choose which fast foods they like, such as pizza, tacos, hamburgers, ice cream, or french fries. Then have the caller shout out those food names instead of numbers.

balloon around

Best For: Second through sixth grade
Energy Level: High
Supplies: *Lots* of balloons

THE GAME:

This game is active, exciting, and great for action photographs of your group at play.

Before the game, blow up one balloon for each player.

Form three groups of equal size and have each stand in a different corner of the room. Pile the balloons in group one's corner.

Instruct kids in group one to carry the balloons under their chins to group two. Have kids in group two remove the balloons from group one by using only their elbows, then carry the balloons with their elbows to group three. Have kids in group three carry the balloons between their knees to the last corner and drop them there.

If kids drop balloons during the game, group members may help them. Play this relay game again and switch roles so the groups carry balloons in different ways. When you're done playing, use the balloons for another game or let everyone have fun popping them.

plastic peanuts

Best For: All ages
Energy Level: Medium
Supplies: Plastic-foam packing "peanuts," two empty boxes, and a watch with a second hand

THE GAME:

Have fun using recyclables to play an exciting game.

Place a large box of plastic-foam packing "peanuts" at one end of the room. Set an empty box at the opposite end of the room.

Form groups of five. Have kids race to carry peanuts from the full container to the empty one. Direct kids to balance the peanuts on their heads, elbows, shoulders, or noses. If a peanut falls off, have the child stop and pick it up then begin again.

Time the group's effort at getting all the peanuts across the room, then have them repeat the game in the other direction, trying to beat their own time.

For a fun variation with younger kids, play Peanut Push Relay. Have kids push peanuts with their noses from one end of the room to the other.

hoop holders

Best For: First through sixth grade
Energy Level: Medium
Supplies: Masking tape, markers, and a plastic hoop for every six players (optional: a watch with a second hand)

THE GAME:

This game gets more exciting—and funnier to watch—each time you play. This game is best played with at least 18 kids.

Put a piece of masking tape on each plastic hoop for a "name tag." Have children stand in a circle, and hand a hoop to every sixth player around the circle. Label each plastic hoop by writing the name of each "hoop holder" on the masking tape of the hoop he or she is holding. Have everyone join hands. Instruct hoop holders to grasp the hands of their neighbors through their hoops. Tell the group to pass the hoops around the circle without letting go of hands.

Encourage players to try different strategies to help each other, such as lifting or lowering the hoop for each other. When all hoops have returned to their hoop holders, instruct players to repeat the sequence in the other direction.

To make it a little more interesting, get a watch with a second hand and play against the clock. Let kids try to improve their time.

flying-disk dodge

Best For: Third through sixth grade
Energy Level: High
Supplies: A flying disk

THE GAME:

Bring out the flying disk—we've got a new game!
Before the game, divide a large rectangular playing area in half with a center line. Form two groups. Have each group choose a side and spread out in that area, facing the opposite group.

Have a player in group one throw a flying disk at a player in group two. If group two doesn't catch the flying disk but a member is hit with it, that player joins group one. If the player catches the flying disk, he or she may throw it at group one. If the flying disk is thrown out of play, have a leader toss it back into play. Have kids continue playing until only one player is left in one of the groups. Caution kids to keep on their toes and watch for the flying disks. Encourage kids to toss the disks at or below waist level for safety.

For older kids, add a fun twist and have them try hopping while they play. Younger children can enjoy this game by using a soft playground ball instead of a flying disk.

the three musketeers

Best For: All ages
Energy Level: Medium
Supplies: None

THE GAME:

One for all and all for one! This game encourages an attitude of cooperation.

Form groups of three and tell kids to prepare to work together. Have kids in each trio link arms. Tell kids to complete the following tasks while joined to their partners. Here are some possible tasks:

● scratch your ears,
● touch your toes,
● take four steps to the right,

- lift one leg,
- sit down,
- stand up,
- bend over and raise your arms, and
- do windmills with your arms.

This game lets kids find ways to cooperate and rely on one another. After giving kids two tasks, have them change groups, allowing everyone a chance to get better acquainted. As a reward for working together, have the kids give themselves a round of applause ... while still linking arms! If you're having refreshments, let them try to eat while in their "musketeer" groups.

box ball

Best For: First through sixth grade
Energy Level: Medium
Supplies: A beach ball, a large box, and masking tape

THE GAME:

This game works best for a group of three to six children. If you have a large group, form smaller groups; the more groups you have, the more fun the game.

Before playing, tape a 4x4-foot square on the floor. Set a large box in the center of the square. Be sure the box is open so a beach ball can be tossed inside.

Have kids stand around the square facing one another. Explain to kids that they'll volley a beach ball to each player, then volley the ball into the box. A player may hit the ball more than once, but each player around the square must volley at least once before they bop the ball into the box.

Increase the challenge by having players stand farther away from the box, by using a smaller ball, or by using two balls.

blanket bounce

Best For: First through sixth grade
Energy Level: Medium
Supplies: Two blankets and a playground ball

THE GAME:

This game is perfect during a lock-in when you're sure to have plenty of blankets.

Before the game, lay two blankets on the floor a few feet apart. Have children form two groups around the edges of the blankets. Instruct children to grasp the edges of their blankets, holding them waist-high. Curl up the edges of the blankets to adjust for smaller groups. Place the playground ball in the center of one blanket and have the group holding that blanket try to toss the ball in the air so the other group can make a "blanket catch."

Encourage the receiving group to let the blanket have extra slack in the middle to make the catch. Allow players to catch the ball off a bounce or on a fly, depending on ability. When the ball is caught, have the receiving group take a step backward before tossing the ball back to the other group. As you play, both groups will gradually get farther apart.

Let kids practice catching a couple of times, then add a new dimension by having them count or say the alphabet while tossing the ball. For more fun with a large group, add more blankets and see how long you can keep the ball going around from one group to another.

countdown balloon

Best For: Kindergarten through second grade
Energy Level: Medium
Supplies: Balloons

THE GAME:

This game has its ups and downs, but it's a lot of fun! You'll need one balloon to play with and extras in case you have a blowout.

Invite the group to stand in a large circle. Choose one player to be "It" and to stand in the center of the circle, holding the balloon. Ask kids to count off until everyone has a number.

Have It throw the balloon up in the air and call out a number. Have the person with that number try to catch the balloon before it touches the ground. If the balloon isn't caught, that person becomes the next It.

If you have a large group of older children, you can have them count off by fives. For example, when It calls for the threes, have everyone with that number hop for the balloon. To add a fun twist, have It call out different ways to get the balloon, such as crawling, walking backward, hopping, or skipping.

You can keep playing until all the balloons are flat or all the kids in the group are flat on their backs!

swamp thing

Best For: All ages
Energy Level: High
Supplies: Balloons and masking tape

THE GAME:

Make sure you have plenty of room to play this game; swamps are big, you know.

Before the game, create a "swamp area" by marking off a 6-foot circle on the floor with masking tape. When you're ready to begin the game, invite kids to enter the swamp. Toss a balloon into the swamp. Encourage kids to keep the balloon in the marked area and off the ground as they bop it back and forth. The first time the balloon falls into the swamp (on the floor), kids go deeper into the swamp by getting on their knees. The next time the balloon touches the floor, have kids get on their bottoms. The next time the balloon touches the floor, let kids lie on their backs. When the balloon hits the ground again, the game is over.

For more excitement, play with more than one balloon.

hug bug

Best For: Second through sixth grade
Energy Level: High
Supplies: None

THE GAME:

This silly game will drive your kids "buggy" with delight.

Form two groups and have them stand at one end of the room. Have each group choose one person to be the "buggy body." The rest of the kids will be the buggy legs. Instruct the buggy legs to kneel side by side. Then have the buggy body lay across the backs of the buggy legs.

On "go," the giant "bugs" will crawl to the other side of the room. When one bug reaches the wall, have those kids give each other a quick group hug then quickly form another bug with a new person as the buggy body. Have kids continue going back and forth until everyone has had a turn to be the buggy body.

When kids are cooling down, point out how everyone helped carry each other. Explain that Jesus wants us to help carry each other's problems and worries, too.

cottoN-ball express

Best For: All ages
Energy Level: High
Supplies: A bag of cotton balls, several emery boards, clothes-pins, drinking straws, a bowl, and a watch with a second hand

THE GAME:

This game's a great way to show your group how quickly they can "pick up" a room.

Scatter all of the cotton balls around the room. Distribute emery boards, clothespins, and drinking straws, allowing one item per child. Place a bowl in the middle of the room.

Demonstrate how to pick up a cotton ball by pinching it with a clothespin, snagging it with an emery board, or sucking it up with a straw. Let kids practice their "techniques," then say "go" and have children scramble to put all the cotton balls in the bowl. Time the kids, then let them try again to improve their time. Allow kids to exchange items before they play again. Provide new straws for round two.

For a variation, let older students pair up and give them one straw apiece. Have kids use the straws as cooperative chopsticks.

rompin' rummage relay

Best For: All ages
Energy Level: High
Supplies: Dress-up items and paper grocery sacks

THE GAME:

Kids love to dress up. This game combines the fun of costumes with the excitement of a relay.

Before the game, gather dress-up items such as old shoes, belts, jackets, shirts, gloves, and scarves. Place the same number of dress-up items in each of two paper grocery sacks.

Invite kids to form small groups and have the groups form lines at one end of the room. Hand the first person in each line a grocery sack containing costume pieces. On "go," have the first child in each group carry his or her bag to the opposite end of the room then put on the costume pieces in the bag. When kids are dressed up, direct them to hop back to their groups and remove their costumes, and have the next person in each line go to the other end of the room and dress up.

Continue until everyone's had a turn to dress up.

balloon blowup

Best For: Second through sixth grade
Energy Level: Medium
Supplies: Small balloons in a variety of colors (four or five of
                   each color) and masking tape

THE GAME:

Before the game, use masking tape to mark starting and finish lines. Half of a marked volleyball or basketball court works well.

Form groups of four or five. Give children in each group small balloons of the same color. Do not blow up the balloons. Have groups line up single file behind the starting line. Instruct the first child in each group to blow up his or her balloon and let it go without tying it. Have the next child stand where the first balloon landed then blow up his or her balloon and let it go. Continue playing until one of the balloons makes it across the finish line. When one group reaches the finish line, have the group turn around and begin again.

To add a challenge, have kids try to get balloons across the line in 30 seconds. Balloons are unpredictable, so this game equalizes athletic and nonathletic kids. Be sure to pick up any balloon pieces if there's a blowout.

human tick-tack-toe

Best For: Third through sixth grade
Energy Level: Medium
Supplies: Masking tape

THE GAME:

Before playing, use masking tape to form large Tick-Tack-Toe boards, one per team. Make the squares on the gameboard one foot square or larger.

Ask kids to form groups of six. Have half of each group choose to be X's and have the other half be O's. Instead of drawing X's and O's, the kids will be making X's and O's with their bodies. Tell the X's to stand with their arms crisscrossed in front of them. The O's will stand with their arms forming big circles. When children are familiar with how to stand, invite them to play Tick-Tack-Toe, deciding as groups where to play the X's and O's.

Try the following variations for fun.

● Blindfold all but two children in each group. Instruct these two players to use their teammates as markers as they play the game, gently guiding them into position. Let children take turns directing the game.

● Play Toe-Tack-Tick. The object is to *not* get three in a row. Have the first player stand in the middle square, giving the other team a slight disadvantage. This takes a little more thinking, but kids will love the challenge.

paper-plate push

Best For: First through third grade
Energy Level: High
Supplies: Four paper plates, large marshmallows, pens, and a pie tin

THE GAME:

Distribute one large marshmallow and a pen to each child. Have kids carefully write their names on the marshmallows. Then gather the marshmallows and put them in a pie tin in the middle of the playing area.

Form four groups and have them line up in the four corners of the room. Give the first person in each group a paper plate. Dump the marshmallows on the floor and instruct the first person from each group—when you say "go"—to capture a marshmallow that belongs to someone in another group. Have each child scoop up a marshmallow then run back to the group. Have each player hold onto the marshmallow he or she captured then hand the plate to the next person in line. Have kids continue playing until each child has captured a marshmallow.

Have kids give friendly pats on the back or handshakes to the people whose names are on their marshmallows. Collect the marshmallows, then have kids play again.

Serve fresh marshmallows as a treat after you're done playing!

smugglers

Best For: All ages
Energy Level: High
Supplies: Masking tape, 10 paper cups, and a watch with a second hand

THE GAME:

What a great way to have fun while helping kids think of faraway brothers and sisters who long for the Word of God.

Before the game, place a strip of masking tape at each end of the playing area. Place another piece of tape in the center of the room and set 10 paper cups on it. Tell kids that the paper cups represent Bibles and that the lines by the walls are people who want to read the Bibles. Explain that the object of the game is to smuggle the paper-cup Bibles over the lines by the walls.

Form two groups: the smugglers and the guards. Have the guards stand by the tape lines at the ends of the playing area. Have the smugglers stand around the center area. On "go," smugglers run to deliver paper cups over the guards' lines. If smugglers are tagged by guards, they must put their cups back. Challenge kids to see if they can get all the cups over the lines in two minutes. Have the smugglers and the guards switch roles and play again.

Try these exciting variations:

● make a "river" by placing two lines of masking tape about two feet apart for kids to jump over while carrying the Bibles,

● direct kids to tiptoe while carrying Bibles so they don't wake the border guards, and

● have kids crawl through the jungle to smuggle their Bibles.

This is a great way to start a discussion about the need for God's Word all over the world.

lifesavers

Best For: First through sixth grade
Energy Level: Medium
Supplies: Life Savers candy (any flavor)

THE GAME:

If you've ever been lost at sea, you know how important a life preserver can be.

Have kids scatter around the room. Call out a number between one and the number of kids in your group. Direct kids to make life preservers by forming groups of the requested number of people. Instruct kids to make a life preserver by putting their arms around each other's shoulders, form-

ing rings. Call the numbers quickly so kids have to hurry to make life preservers. You don't want anyone to sink at sea! If kids can't form a group
with the correct number, encourage them to make a smaller preserver.
Call out the number of kids in your group for the last life preserver.

Share Life Savers candy when the game is over.

zigzag

Best For: All ages
Energy Level: Medium
Supplies: Paper cups and small wads of paper

THE GAME:

If you've been saving newspapers, here's a great way to use some of them.
Invite the kids to form two groups. Have groups stand in two lines, six
feet apart, facing each other so that each person has a partner across
from him or her. Hand a paper cup to each person. Give a small wad of
paper to the first person in one of the lines. The object of the game is to
toss the wad back and forth in a zigzag pattern down the lines. If the kids
are unable to get the ball all the way down the lines, have them start from
the other end and try again. With a little practice and cooperation, the kids
will get the hang of it!

For more fun, try this with two paper wads coming from different directions.

indoor olympics

Best For: Kindergarten through third grade
Energy Level: Medium
Supplies: Drinking straws, paper plates, plastic hoops, a bal-
                   loon or a playground ball, masking tape, chilled
                   apple juice, and three-ring pretzels

THE GAME:

Have Olympic-sized fun with these goofy games.
Tell kids to form pairs or trios and decide on crazy team names.
Then let the teams rotate among the events.

● Toss-a-Round: Tape a tossing line on the floor with masking tape.
Have kids toss a paper-plate "discus." Let kids count the number of steps

the discus lands from the tossing line.

● Heave-Ho: Have kids see how far they can toss drinking-straw "javelins."

● Crab Dash: Have one partner "crab walk" around the room one time while the other partner cheers him or her on. Then have partners switch roles.

● Hoop-It-Up: One partner holds a plastic hoop while the other partner tries to make a basket by tossing a balloon or a playground ball through the hoop. Have kids switch places so each partner has a chance to be a basketball "superstar."

End your Olympic fun with chilled apple juice and three-ring pretzels.

friendly fanning

Best For: All ages
Energy Level: High
Supplies: Paper plates, balloons, and a watch with a second hand

THE GAME:

This is a great way to cool off, and it's a lot cheaper than air conditioning!

Before this activity, blow up a balloon for each player.

Form pairs and give each person a paper plate. Have pairs line up at one end of the room. Give a balloon to the first pair. Show kids how to use their paper plates as fans to keep the balloon in the air. On "go," have the first pair work together to fan the balloon to the other side of the room, bounce it off the wall, then fan it back to the next pair without letting it touch the floor. Keep track of the time. Continue play until everyone has had a chance to fan a balloon across the room. Have kids change partners and try again to improve their time.

For a fun variation, have kids form a circle and keep a few balloons in the air with their fans. Keep adding balloons to see how many they can keep airborne simultaneously.

hot-air balloon

Best For: First through sixth grade
Energy Level: Medium
Supplies: Plenty of balloons, masking tape, and a watch with a second hand

THE GAME:

Before the game, use masking tape to mark off a large X or Y shape. Form three or four groups. Have kids kneel with their hands behind their backs, one group in each of the marked areas. Explain that each group's goal is to blow balloons into other groups' areas.

On "go," drop several balloons into play. Encourage kids to blow the balloons to their opponents' sides. Call time at one minute and let kids count to see how many balloons are in their areas.

As kids get the idea, add more balloons. For another twist, try cotton balls. No matter what you use, it's a great way for kids to blow off some steam and extra energy.

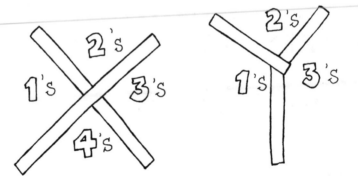

tag and toss

Best For: All ages
Energy Level: High
Supplies: Lightweight objects such as balls of yarn, table tennis balls, or paper wads

THE GAME:

Here's a fun twist on Tag. This game keeps kids moving and working with their partners.

Ask the group to form pairs. Select one pair to be taggers. Give each of the other pairs a different lightweight object. You may choose paper wads of different colors, marked balls, or a mixture of objects. Tell the children they're safe from the taggers if they're holding their objects. Since each pair has to share its object, encourage kids to look out for each other. On "go," have the group begin running around the room as the taggers try to catch them. Direct kids to throw their objects back and forth with their partners to prevent being caught. If one partner is tagged, then both become the new taggers and give their object to the original pair of taggers.

This one will wear out the most energetic of groups (or at least the leaders).

Mummies

Best For: Third through sixth grade
Energy Level: Medium
Supplies: Two rolls of gauze or crepe paper

THE GAME:

This game combines the excitement of a relay race with one of the great unanswered questions of all time: Why do children love to run in circles?

Have kids form two groups and have each group stand in a line at one end of the room. Be sure the lines are facing each other. Hand the first child in one line a roll of gauze or crepe paper and the last child in the other line a roll of gauze or crepe paper. Tell kids they're going to make crazy mummies by wrapping and unwrapping each other. On "go," have the kids with the gauze or crepe paper wrap up like mummies the kids beside them in line. Then the mummies must hop across the room to the opposite line, where the first (and last) kids in line can unwrap the mummies and use the gauze or crepe paper to wrap the kids next in line. Play the game a few times, scrambling the line order each time.

Continue playing until each child has had a turn to be a mummy.

airplaNe affirmatioNs

Best For: First through sixth grade
Energy Level: Medium
Supplies: Paper, markers, and a stapler

THE GAME:

This game is fun and is a great way to make your kids feel like flying. Form a circle. If you have a large group, form circles with 10 members in each. Give each child a marker and enough paper to make one note for each person in his or her circle.

Have kids each write an encouraging note to each person in the circle. These can simply say, "John, thanks for coming today" or "Kya, you have a terrific smile." Younger kids who can't write well may draw simple pictures. Be sure that kids write the other students' names on top to guarantee airmail delivery! When kids have finished writing, instruct them to take off their right shoes and place them in front of them. Demonstrate how to make a simple paper airplane, and have kids make their notes into airplanes. Encourage kids to help one another as they fold their notes into airplanes. Have kids take turns "flying" their airplane affirmations to each other's shoes.

After the air has cleared, give kids a few moments to gather and read their encouraging notes. Staple the pages together so kids can take their affirmations home.

ballooN blastoff

Best For: First through third grade
Energy Level: Medium
Supplies: An old sheet, inflated balloons, and markers

THE GAME:

This game makes a great crowd-breaker and helps kids learn each other's names at the start of the year.

Place the old sheet in the middle of the playing area. Give each person a balloon and a marker. Instruct kids to write their names on the balloons.

Form two groups. Have group one gather around the sheet, with each person holding an edge. Place all of the balloons on the sheet. Have the other group scatter around the room. On "go," group one pulls the sheet tight, causing the balloons to launch into the air. Group one then drops the sheet and runs with group two to catch the balloons. If kids grab their own balloons, tell them to drop them and grab other ones. Once each child has caught a balloon with someone else's name on it, have him or her find that person and complete the sentence "Hi! My name is ___, and I'm glad you're here today because..."

Play again and let the other group be the balloon launchers. Continue playing until each group has held the sheet two times.

• •

raft ride

Best For:　　　First through sixth grade
Energy Level:　Medium
Supplies:　　　Old newspapers and masking tape

THE GAME:

Land ho! This game will shape up your shipmates.

Form groups of four called crews. Give each crew four sheets of newspaper and a few pieces of masking tape. Tell each crew to build a raft by taping its four sheets of newspaper together. When the rafts are done, set them on one side of the room. Have crews stand or sit on their rafts then "sail" the rafts across the floor by scooting the paper. This requires a cooperative effort!

After the group completes a few "ocean voyages," have the crews decide what each of their members did best on their voyages, such as planning, listening, moving paper, taking orders, or giving instructions.

Make sure to take any extra paper to a recycling center or save it for craft projects in class.

balloon sweep

Best For: Fourth through sixth grade
Energy Level: Medium
Supplies: Balloons and paper plates

THE GAME:

This game works best with lots of kids.

Choose five or six kids to be human obstacles in an obstacle course. Hand the obstacles each a paper plate and have them stand scattered around the playing area.

Form two groups with the rest of the kids and hand them each a balloon. Have the kids stand at one end of the playing area. Explain that the object of the game is for the kids to move from one end of the playing area to the other, batting the balloons and going in and out and around the obstacles. The obstacles will move their arms and wave the paper plates to create breezes to blow the balloons off course. Have the kids work their way through the obstacle course a few times, then choose new kids to be the obstacles.

For a fun twist, see if pairs of kids with arms interlocked can each maneuver two balloons around the obstacles.

froggy

Best For: Second through sixth grade
Energy Level: Medium
Supplies: Gummie Worms candy

THE GAME:

Make sure your group number is divisible by three, because there are three parts to a frog.

Demonstrate the posture for each part: the kids representing the legs squat with knees extended, kids who represent heads place their hands on their ears with their elbows sticking straight out, and the kids who represent arms stand with their arms extended at the shoulders.

Encourage kids on "go" to assume one of the three body positions. Then have them try to match up with others as quickly as possible to form complete bodies—legs first, then heads and arms. Kids have to cooperate to make complete frogs. Encourage kids to communicate by saying, "This frog needs a head!" or "Where are the frog legs?" Have kids play until everyone has helped to form a complete frog.

For a greater challenge, have kids "connect" with different people for each round. Have them keep trying until frogs are everywhere! Then have them jump across the gym for Gummie Worms treats.

outdoor games

An Introduction to Outdoor Games

There's something about playing outside that nurtures fun and fellowship among kids. Smiles are brighter and games more exciting when kids play in the sunshine. Whether you have a gigantic churchyard or just a small back lot, use the games in this section to have some sunny-day fun.

three squirts and you're out

Best For: All ages
Energy Level: High
Supplies: Red construction paper, scissors, small squirt guns, and a bucket of water

THE GAME:

Be sure kids wear old clothes or clothes that can get damp during the squirty fun.

Before this game, cut 3×4-inch strips of red construction paper to represent candles. Cut out six candles. Fill a bucket with water, then fill small squirt guns for half the kids in your group.

Form two groups: the "squirters" and the "savers." Have the squirters form two lines facing each other, about six feet apart. Give each of the squirters a full squirt gun. Position the savers at the far end of the playing field and have them choose a person to be the candleholder. Hand the candleholder a red construction paper candle and tell him or her to hold the candle in the air. Then tell the savers to form a tight circle around the candleholder.

On "go," have the savers and the candleholder walk between the lines of squirters. The squirters try to "extinguish" the paper candle by hitting it with water. When three hits are made, have the squirters shout, "You're out!" Then have the groups switch roles. Each group will get five chances to let its little light shine!

SQUIRTERS

SAVERS

cookie stackers

Best For: All ages
Energy Level: Medium
Supplies: Sugar cookies, an old sheet, canned frosting, paper plates, a cookie sheet, craft sticks, and a watch with a second hand

THE GAME:

This game is a fun way to prepare treats for your group — and for grateful birds!

Before the game, spread an old sheet on the ground. Set out canned frosting and sugar cookies on a cookie sheet. Form several small groups and hand each group a paper plate and a craft stick. Position the groups about 20 feet away from the cookies.

On "go," have the first person from each group hold the craft stick and hop to the cookies. That player picks up a cookie and a "dip" of frosting, returns to the group, places the cookie on the paper plate, and frosts the cookie. Then the next person in line hops up for another cookie and a dip of frosting. Have kids continue stacking cookies for one minute or until each person has had a turn, whichever comes first.

Combine cookie towers on the cookie sheet, then have everyone help gobble down the goodies!

Here's a challenging variation that requires more cooperation: Have each participant work with one arm behind his or her back.

wet and wild walkin'

Best For: Kindergarten through sixth grade
Energy Level: High
Supplies: Paper cups and water

THE GAME:

This game is a wild, wet experience and is best played on a hot summer day. Have kids wear old clothes they won't mind getting wet.

Before the game, have the group choose a bush or tree to represent a finish line. Invite children to form pairs, and have partners stand shoulder to shoulder. Place a paper cup of water between the shoulders of each pair. Partners walk to the finish line while trying not to spill their water. After everyone reaches the finish line, have children check each other's cups to see how much water is left.

Try these variations:
- walking with the water cup between partners' knees,
- walking with the water cup between partners' noses,
- walking with the water cup between partners' heads, and
- walking with the water cup between partners' stomachs.

the blob

Best For: All ages
Energy Level: High
Supplies: None

THE GAME:

This game adds a new twist to Tag and gets your group to "stick together."
Select a "tagger" for this high-energy game. That person may tag any one's shoulder with his or her hand but must continue holding on. As each person is tagged, he or she becomes part of the "blob" and must travel with the original tagger to touch someone else's shoulder. Only the tagger may tag other players. The last person tagged becomes the next tagger. For a twist, change from tagging shoulders to tagging hands, elbows, knees, or backs.

As a variation, allow the tagger to choose to be a dog (running on hands and knees), a kangaroo (hopping on two feet), or a horse (running on two feet as in regular Tag). The entire blob must imitate the animal the tagger chooses. If you're a leader hoping to sit this one out, watch out! The blob may get you, too!

chip off the old block

Best For: Third through sixth grade
Energy Level: Low
Supplies: Plaster of Paris, plastic knives and spoons, 3×5 cards, pens, medium-sized rocks, and an empty plastic yogurt container or a small paper milk carton for each pair of kids

THE GAME:

This game may take a little more preparation than some, but it's an awesome way to get kids to "chip" in as they create fun sculptures.

Two days before this activity, mix the plaster of Paris according to the package directions and pour the plaster into empty plastic yogurt containers or small paper milk cartons. Let the plaster harden completely.

Form pairs and give each pair a block of plaster (still in the container), a plastic knife and spoon, a 3×5 card, a pen, and a medium-sized rock. Tell kids to remove the plaster from the containers. Kids may need help in getting the plaster out. Demonstrate how to turn a container over and shake the plaster out into an open hand. If they are using milk cartons, have kids peel the paper off the plaster.

Explain that kids will work together to prepare sculptures for an art show. Allow partners two minutes to decide what they'll sculpt and how they'll go about it. Have kids begin sculpting when you say "go." Plan for at least 10 minutes of sculpting time. Tell kids to use the rocks and the plastic knives to chisel. As kids finish, have them place their works of art on a table, along with 3×5 cards that state the titles of the pieces.

If the plaster breaks during the process of sculpting, encourage students to create several small sculptures. When everyone has finished, invite each pair of artists to present its masterpiece and to tell about the item. Leave the sculptures on display as reminders of how beautiful it is when kids work together.

dash 'N' splash

Best For: Second through sixth grade
Energy Level: High
Supplies: Paper cups, a water supply, two buckets, and a piece of string

THE GAME:

The real goal of this game is to cool off a hot group.

On a hot day, have the group dress in swimsuits or clothes they don't mind getting wet. Use a piece of string to mark a center line in your playing area. Form two groups and have them stand on opposing sides of the center line. Designate one group as the "splashers" and the other as the "dashers." Give each person a paper cup and hand each group a bucket full of water. Tell groups to place the water buckets at the back of their areas.

Explain that when you say, "Splash time!" both groups are to dip their cups into their water, toss the water on their opponents, then run back for water refills. Have them continue until one group empties its water bucket or until everyone feels cool.

squirrels

Best For: Kindergarten through second grade
Energy Level: Medium
Supplies: Peanuts in the shell, napkins, and a watch with a
                   second hand

THE GAME:

This game may seem a little nutty, but it teaches cooperation and it's a lot of fun.

Before the game, scatter peanuts over a large grassy area. Have kids form pairs, linking arms. Let kids choose to be "squirrels" or "trees." Explain that the squirrels gather the nuts and the trees store the nuts. Allow each pair to take one napkin and place it away from the main playing area. The napkin is the nest. When a pair finds a peanut, direct the squirrel to grab it and hand it to the tree. Both run to stash it in the nest. The goal is for pairs to find as many peanuts as they can in three minutes.

To make things a little more "squirrelly," vary the ways squirrels hunt for peanuts, such as crawling, hopping, or skipping. Don't worry if you leave a few peanuts behind—*real* squirrels will take care of them!

cookie capers

Best For: Kindergarten through sixth grade
Energy Level: High
Supplies: A plate of cookies

THE GAME:

This is a fun way to get ready for treats.

Fill a plate with enough cookies for your entire group. Play this game in a grassy area. Put the plate of cookies at one end of the playing area. Have the group form pairs and stand at the opposite end of the playing area. Ask an adult leader to be the "caller." Instruct the caller to call out actions for pairs to carry out. Tell kids to listen closely and follow the caller's instructions to work their way to the cookies. Let pairs take turns moving to the plate of cookies.

Here are a few suggestions:

● **Action 1—Wheelbarrow:** Have one child put his or her hands on the ground, keeping legs straight. The other child stands at the first child's feet and lifts them up, tucking them under his or her arms. The wheelbarrow moves forward by hand and by foot.

● **Action 2—Arm Lock:** Have partners sit on the ground back-to-back and lock their arms together. Challenge them to try to stand up by pushing against one another. Have them walk back to back with arms locked.

● **Action 3—Twirlers:** Instruct partners to face each other and hold hands, crisscrossing their arms. Have them turn circles under each other's arms so their arms become uncrossed.

For fun, let the caller make up new actions involving the partners. Have kids continue playing until everyone is waiting at the cookie plate. Then celebrate your cooperative victory by eating all the cookies.

grass grab

Best For: All ages
Energy Level: Medium
Supplies: A large grassy area

THE GAME:

This game works best when played in an area that really needs mowing. The longer the grass, the more fun the game is.

Start with everyone outside in a large grassy playing area. Have each child pick one blade of grass and hold one end of it. Have one child volunteer to be the leader. Direct the leader to link up with someone by holding the other end of a child's blade of grass. Then have the two connect to the rest of the group, everyone holding on to the blades of grass. Challenge the group to move around the playing area, in circles, and around trees, staying in a chain held together by blades of grass. When the line or a blade of grass breaks, begin a new game with a new leader.

If you play long enough, no one will have to mow the grass!

crossing the chasm

Best For: Second through sixth grade
Energy Level: Medium
Supplies: One 6-foot piece of 2x4 lumber and a watch with a second hand

THE GAME:

Kids will want to try this game over and over again.

Before the game, place the six-foot piece of 2x4 lumber in the center of the playing area. Invite kids to form two groups. Have each group stand at one end of the 2x4. Tell kids that this board is a bridge over a huge chasm. The object of the game is to get the groups to trade places by crossing the bridge without falling off. This takes tremendous teamwork. Have two people meet halfway across the bridge. Encourage them to hold hands for balance as they pass each other by trading positions. If someone falls, have him or her go to the back of the line to try again. Play until everyone has crossed the chasm safely. Keep track of the time and play again to let kids try to improve their time.

To play inside, simply place two six-foot strips of tape four inches apart in the center of the room. No matter where you play, this game will help your group work together and have fun while they cooperate.

recycle-rama

Best For: All ages
Energy Level: High
Supplies: Masking tape and recyclables (cardboard boxes, empty paper-towel rolls, empty milk cartons, newspapers)

THE GAME:

This activity brings out the creativity in a group; plus it's a lot of fun to use in conjunction with a recycling drive.

Place all the recyclables in the center of the playing area. Have the class form three groups. Allow the groups to take turns choosing items from the supply of recyclables. Once the supply is exhausted, give groups three minutes to think of games to play with the recyclables. Spark ideas with these possibilities: Use an empty paper-towel roll as a bat and wadded newspaper as a ball; use a cardboard box as a basket and empty milk cartons as balls;

roll up newspapers to form short ropes for one-on-one Tugs of War.

Have the three groups demonstrate their games to the rest of the class. Then let each group rotate to the next game until everyone has played each game.

Not only will you be environmentally correct, but you'll have fun, too.

hankie handoff

Best For: First through sixth grade
Energy Level: Medium
Supplies: Two to four handkerchiefs

THE GAME:

This is a great game to help kids burn off energy.

Form two groups and have them stand opposite each other 10 feet apart. Help each group number off from the beginning to the end of its line.

Stand between the two groups and hold two handkerchiefs. Toss up the hankies and call out a number within the range of numbers represented in the groups. The two players with that number each hop on one foot to pick up a hankie, then take it back to the team. Then the first player passes the hankie over his or her head to the next player, who passes the hankie under his or her knees to the next player. The hankies proceed to the end of the lines in this under-and-over pattern. Have the last person in each line hop the hankie back to you, and begin the relay again.

For added fun, use four hankies and call out two numbers simultaneously.

LEADER

trash 'N' trade

Best For: Second through sixth grade
Energy Level: High
Supplies: Trash cans or trash bags

THE GAME:

This is a game to play at a park or playground. Be sure there are trash cans scattered around the park or play area. If not, you may want to bring your own trash bags and scatter them around the area.

Form pairs. On "go," have one player from each pair touch a trash can while his or her partner runs to pick up a piece of trash. As the runners throw the trash into the cans, instruct them to tag their partners and reverse roles. Have kids keep playing until the area is clean.

To play this game in groups, assign a trash can to each group. Have half of each group run for trash while the other half waits at the trash can. As the runners toss the trash, they tag their partners, who continue the cleanup. This game is fun for your group, and the results are fun for others as they enjoy the area you made beautiful!

After the game, take a breather and talk about beautiful places the kids have visited and what made these places special. Point out that parks and playgrounds need special care to keep them inviting and nice.

bandanna bandits

Best For: Second through sixth grade
Energy Level: High
Supplies: Two bandannas

THE GAME:

This game burns up lots of energy! So play it when your kids can't seem to sit still.

Invite kids to form two equal groups. Instruct them to stand in a single file line. Have each child hold the waist of the child in front of him or her. Give a bandanna to the last child in each line. Have them tuck the bandannas into their pockets or waistbands so the bandannas hang down like tails.

Encourage the first players, and *only* the first players in each line, to run and try to get the bandanna from the end of the other line. The first player in each line is the "bandanna bandit." Tell the other kids to follow the leader, holding on to the people in front of them. Each team may dodge and run to protect its bandanna. When the bandanna is taken, have the last person move to the front. Attach the bandanna to the new end person. Have kids play until they drop along with the bandannas.

whirlpool

Best For: Third through sixth grade
Energy Level: High
Supplies: None

THE GAME:

Players in this game form human whirlpools. This is a dizzying thought, but kids love it.

Before the game, let kids choose an object to act as the finish line at one end of the playing area. Form groups of five to seven players. Have groups stand in single file lines at the other end of the playing area, facing the finish line.

On "go," have the first child in each line run in a circle around his or her group. As the player passes the front of the line, direct the second child to grab the first child's belt or waist from behind. Then the two players run in a circle around the group. Continue until all the players in each group are linked. When the last child has joined the whirlpool, the line leader heads for the finish line. The whirlpool will straighten out as it crosses the finish line.

Let the first whirlpool to finish choose the next game.

beetles and beavers

Best For: All ages
Energy Level: High
Supplies: None

THE GAME:

Here is a game that sharpens listening skills by building suspense. And when the suspense is broken, play turns into a raucous game of group Tag.

Have children form two groups: the "beetles" and the "beavers." Have the groups line up on starting lines at opposite ends of the playing area, facing each other. Have an adult leader stand in the middle of the field.

When the leader gives a signal, the two groups begin moving toward each other. Meanwhile, have the leader begin to call out the name of one of the groups, the beetles or the beavers. Allow the group whose name the leader calls to instantly turn back and run to the safety of its starting line. Direct the other group to chase the running kids, trying to tag them before they reach the line. If kids are tagged, they join the other group.

After the game is over, see if the leader can say a few tongue twisters to get back to normal!

• •

sock it to Me

Best For: Second through sixth grade
Energy Level: Medium
Supplies: Several old socks

THE GAME:

Here's a game to play with kids who know each other's names.

Before the game, make old socks into balls by rolling them up and tucking the extra fabric around to hold them in shape.

Gather kids in a circle. Tell kids they're going to play a zany game of Memory. Explain that the first time they toss the sock ball to someone, they're to remember who they tossed it to, and for the rest of the game, they're to toss the ball to that same person.

Go slowly until all the kids are familiar with the pattern they've set. Then keep the ball going in the same pattern for a few minutes. Then add another sock ball and keep both going at once in the pattern.

See how many sock balls older kids can keep in play while maintaining the pattern.

Don't watch this game too closely from the sidelines—it will make you dizzy.

true-false tag

Best For: First through sixth grade
Energy Level: High
Supplies: String or masking tape

THE GAME:

This is one pop quiz that all your kids will enjoy.

Before the game, use the string or masking tape to make two lines six feet apart in the middle of the playing area. Make another line 30 feet behind each of the first lines.

Form two groups. One group is the "true" group and the other is the "false" group. Have groups stand on the lines in the middle of the playing area. Have an adult leader, standing a step outside of the playing area, call out a statement such as "Birds have wings" or "The sky is green." If the statement is true, the true group runs to its line, chased by the false group, which tries to tag the true group. If the statement is false, have the false group run to its line, chased by the true group. Any players who are tagged join the opposite group.

For older kids, use true and false statements from the Bible. For a change of pace, let group members take turns calling out true or false statements.

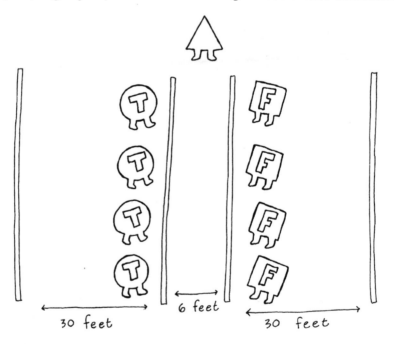

bubble-pop pictures

Best For: All ages
Energy Level: Medium
Supplies: Bubble soap; bubble blowers; old shirts; poster board; masking tape; and red, blue, and green food coloring

THE GAME:

Play this game on a sunny day with little or no wind. It's a lot of fun to watch the bubbles float across a bright blue sky.

Before the game, add two drops of one color of food coloring to each container of prepared bubble soap, or make your own bubbles, using this recipe.

Tape poster board at one end of the playing area on a tree, bush, or chair. Form three groups and have them line up 20 feet from the poster board. Hand an old shirt to the first person in each line. Also give the first person in each line a bubble blower and bubble soap.

> **Bubble Soap**
>
> Fill pie tins or jars each with ½ cup of dish detergent, 1 cup of warm water, 2 to 3 tablespoons of glycerin, and ½ teaspoon of sugar. Add 2 drops of red, blue, or green food coloring to each container.

Explain that kids are to run to the poster board then blow bubbles. When one of their bubbles pops on the poster board, the blower runs back to his or her group and gives the old shirt, bubble soap, and blower to the next person in line.

Continue blowing colorful bubbles until each person has had two turns. Display the "popped picture" in your classroom. Point out that it took everyone's bubble power to make such a beautiful picture.

barrel rolls

Best For: Kindergarten through third grade
Energy Level: High
Supplies: None

THE GAME:

This game is fun to play when everyone is wearing old clothes!

Before the game, have children designate a "roller rink" area. Let kids pick bushes or trees to mark the starting and finish lines at opposite ends of the playing area.

Have each child choose a partner. Let players in each pair choose which one will be the "barrel" and which one will be the "roller." Instruct the barrels to lie down parallel to the starting line, then have the rollers stand behind them. On "go," the rollers gently push the barrels over and over across the roller rink. When a pair reaches the finish line, instruct those kids to switch roles and to join with another pair. This time, one of the barrels loosely holds the ankles of the other, forming a double barrel to roll across the rink.

Remind the children that the goal is not speed but is working together to get to the finish line without breaking apart. If you have a slightly inclined area, everyone can be a barrel—no rollers required!

ticklin' toes

Best For: All ages
Energy Level: Low
Supplies: Marbles and a bucket half filled with water

THE GAME:

This is a fun game to play outside on a hot summer day.

Ask kids to each remove one shoe and sock and set them aside. Invite kids to form two groups. Have the groups line up, then place a marble at the front of each line. Make sure the marbles are different colors so the groups don't confuse them. Place a half-filled bucket of water at the opposite end of the playing area.

Have the first kids in line roll, push, or slide their marbles toward the bucket using only their toes. When they reach the bucket, instruct kids to pick up the marbles with their toes and drop them into the bucket, then return to their lines and tap the next players in line. Have the next player in each line run to the bucket and retrieve the marble with his or her toes. Have kids continue dropping and retrieving marbles until everyone in each group has had a turn.

For a toe-ticklin' variation, form two lines and have kids pass marbles to the end of the lines and back.

flying-disk freNZY

Best For: Kindergarten through sixth grade
Energy Level: High
Supplies: A flying disk and a permanent marker

THE GAME:

Here's another variation of Tag, but with a team twist.
    Before this activity, use a permanent marker to draw stars on one side of a flying disk, and stripes on the other side.

Form two groups: the "stars" and the "stripes." Have them stand in straight lines facing each other about four feet apart. Designate the area behind each group as the safety zone. Gently toss the flying disk into the air so it will land between the two groups. If the stars are facing up when it lands, direct the stars to run for their safety zone while the stripes try to tag them. Any player tagged before reaching the safety zone must then join the other group. Play continues until only one player is left on a side.

float frolic

Best For: Second through sixth grade
Energy Level: High
Supplies: Large plastic bowls, drinking straws, root beer, vanilla ice cream, and plastic spoons

THE GAME:

Play this great thirst quencher on a hot summer day.
    Invite kids to form groups of three. Have groups stand in single file lines at one end of the playing area. Hand each child a drinking straw and a plastic spoon. Explain that they're going to have a delicious treat but they'll have to work together with their groups to make the treat disappear! As you explain how the game works, put two or three scoops of vanilla ice cream in each large plastic bowl, then pour root beer over the ice cream, making gigantic root beer floats! Place the bowls 10 feet apart at the end of the playing area opposite the kids.

On "go," let kids run to the bowls and slurp and gobble their way to the bottom. Encourage the groups with silly cheers such as:

Slurp! Slurp! Slurp!
Go! Go! Go!
Yummy-dilly!
Tummy-tilly!
Ho! Ho! Ho!

Be sure to have kids help clean up the area when everyone's ready to "float away."

jUMp-rope jiNgles

Best For: All ages
Energy Level: High
Supplies: A 10-foot length of rope

THE GAME:

Jump-rope rhymes and songs used to be the big thing on the block. Reintroduce this pastime to the children in your group.

Choose two children to turn the 10-foot rope. Have the other children line up a few feet away from the turning rope. Even large groups of children can play in a single jump-rope game if they jump in rounds. The following rhymes will get you started.

Start the rope turning at a steady pace. Have the first child jump as everyone repeats this verse:

Polly put the kettle on,
Kettle on, kettle on.
Polly put the kettle on
To have some tea.

At the word "tea," direct the first child to jump out of the rope and have the second child jump in. The first child then runs around and gets in line again. When children miss, let them hold the ends of the rope.

Be sure to alternate your jump-roping styles so all kids feel comfortable jumping! Try a fun style of swaying the jump-rope back and forth low to the ground. Here's a verse to use:

I like coffee,
I like tea.
I'd like (name of next child in line)
To jump with me.

little squirt

Best For: Kindergarten through third grade
Energy Level: Medium
Supplies: White paper towels; squirt guns; buckets of water; tape; and blue, red, and yellow food coloring

THE GAME:

This game is great fun if kids don't mind a splash of color, but be sure to have kids wear *old clothes* to play.

Before this activity, fill three buckets with water and add a few drops of one color of food coloring to each bucket. Plan to have one squirt gun for each color of water. Fill each squirt gun before the game.

Tape white paper towels to a tree, bush, or old chair. Set the buckets five feet away from the paper towels. Form three groups and have each group line up behind a bucket. Give someone in each group a squirt gun. On "go," that player runs to the paper towels and squirts them once for every year old he or she is. For example, a 7-year-old would squirt the paper towel seven times. When the first three kids have played, gently untape the paper towels and lay them in the sun to dry. Provide fresh paper towels and have kids continue squirting until everyone's had at least one turn.

When the "decorated" paper towels are dry, let kids help you tape them together to form a quilt. Hang the quilt in your church or classroom as a reminder of each special "squirt" in your group!

the blip in the blob

Best For: First through sixth grade
Energy Level: Medium
Supplies: None

THE GAME:

This fun game is best when played in an area with trees, bushes, playground equipment, or other obstacles.

Form groups of five to 10. Have each group form a circle, holding elbows, and choose one player to stand in the center of each circle. The person in the center is the "blip," and the circle is the "blob." Show each blip a course with three or four things to maneuver around, such as slides, trees, bushes, or a picnic table. The blips walk, hop, skip, or jump slowly around the course as the blobs move along and try to keep the blips in the center of the circles. Each blob must copy the blip's movements. Have kids play until you call out, "Blip flip," then have each blob choose another blip to go to the center. There will always be one blip in the center at a time.

Play until everyone has been a blip in the blob.

travel games

An Introduction to Travel Games

Games bring groups together. And what better time for a great game than when you're on your way from here to there? These travel games are guaranteed to provide on-the-move fun and will minimize the number of times you'll hear, "Are we there yet?" So whether you're walking to a local landmark or driving to Kalamazoo, hit the road and have some fun with traveling games!

story signs

Best For: All ages
Energy Level: Low
Supplies: A road map

THE GAME:

On the road again? Remember that there's a story behind every sign.
    On a van or bus trip, choose someone to be the "story starter." Hand the story starter a road map and invite the story starter to begin telling a silly story about your group's trip. For example, the story starter might say, "Once upon a time, seven kids from Colorado were on their way to the amusement park when all of a sudden..." The story starter continues until spotting a billboard or sign. Then he or she incorporates something about that billboard or sign into the story. For instance, the story starter might continue the story with "someone came running out of Joe's Family Diner, screaming, 'The tuna casserole is alive! Run for your life!'" The story starter then passes the map to someone else, who continues telling the story until spying the next billboard. The last person may end the story in a creative way then start a sequel. Only the person holding the map may speak.

Younger children who can't read can look at pictures on billboards and signs to make up a story. And if you have kindergarten kids, encourage them to hunt for letters of the alphabet on billboards.

Moving Motions

Best For: Kindergarten through second grade
Energy Level: Low
Supplies: None

THE GAME:

On your next road trip, try this "moving" game.
Ask kids to think of five things they might see while traveling, such as green cars, fences, bridges, airplanes, horses, or semitrailers. Then have kids design a motion to go with each item, such as honking an imaginary horn for a green car or slapping their knees in a galloping rhythm for a horse. When someone spots one of the items, he or she says the name of that item, then begins doing the appropriate motion while everyone else joins in. Once all the kids are doing the motion, have them stop and keep searching for more objects from the list.

To add a challenging twist, add sound effects for each motion, such as saying, "Vroom, vroom" for green cars. The more items, motions, and sound effects you add, the crazier the game.

rhythm road

Best For: Fourth through sixth grade
Energy Level: Low
Supplies: None

THE GAME:

This rhythm game is fun and easy to play while walking on the way.
Have one child begin by clapping in this rhythm: 1-2, 1-2-3. Have a second child repeat that rhythm—1-2, 1-2-3—and add a stomp with his or her feet: 1-2, 1-2-3, stomp. A third child repeats the sequence then adds a hop: 1-2, 1-2-3, stomp, hop. Have each child repeat the sequence, adding something new.
Suggested actions include
- hopping,
- twirling in a circle,
- touching your toes,
- jumping backward, and
- flapping your arms.

This game is especially fun if your group is hiking or is sitting around a campfire at a church retreat!

who? what? where?

Best For: Third through sixth grade
Energy Level: Low
Supplies: None

THE GAME:

This is a perfect game for long road trips. Make sure you'll be passing lots of billboards and signs along the way.

Encourage kids to work together to answer three questions: Who? What? and Where? Tell them they will use billboards and signs to find the answers. Have kids begin looking for names or pictures of people on signs along the road. As soon as a child spots the "who," have him or her say, "I know the who!" Let the child tell the group who he or she saw. For example, a child may see a billboard with Snoopy on it. Snoopy will be the who. Then have everyone begin looking for the "what." When a child finds a sign describing what Snoopy could be doing, have him or her say, "I found the what" and tell the group what Snoopy is doing. To fill in the last answer, have someone find a sign with a location on it. Have him or her call out, "I found the where!" Now put the whole puzzle together: *Snoopy* is selling *used cars* at *Pizza Patio.*

jump the bump

Best For: All ages
Energy Level: Medium
Supplies: None

THE GAME:

Play this game while on a walking trip.

Form a single file line and choose a "leapin' leader." Encourage the leader to encounter imaginary objects to jump and leap over. When the leader encounters an imaginary bump, he or she shouts, "Jump the bump!" and jumps over it. Everyone in line follows and jumps the imaginary bump.

After the last person in line jumps and shouts, "Jump the bump!" the leader picks a new imaginary object to duck under or crawl over. For example, "duck the dinosaur" or "crawl through the cave." To avoid confusion, the leader should not shout out a new object until the last person in line has repeated the last action. Switch leaders after three calls by having the leader go to the back of the line and a new leader take his or her place.

Play until everyone has been the leader.

dear johN

Best For: Third through sixth grade
Energy Level: Low
Supplies: Paper, 3×5 cards, pencils, and a hat

THE GAME:

This activity gives kids a constructive and fun way to pass time on a long trip.

Before the game, write each child's name on a 3×5 card and place the cards in a hat. Let each child pick one name from the hat. If they draw their own names, have them try again. Pass out paper and a pencil to each child. Have kids write the names of the people from their 3×5 cards at the top of their papers. Then encourage kids to write letters to those people. Challenge them to add information about the trip, funny things that have happened, and hopes for what will happen. Give kids as much time as they need to complete their letters. At the next pit stop, have kids deliver their letters. Then let them write responses to their pen pals.

Nature scavenger hunt

Best For: Kindergarten through third grade
Energy Level: Medium
Supplies: 3x5 cards

THE GAME:

Play this game when you're walking to or from the park.

Form groups of up to five kids. Give each group a 3x5 card with a list of nature items for kids to find, such as a twig, a leaf, two blades of grass, a blue flower, and a brown rock. For younger players, draw pictures of the items to be found.

Challenge kids to look for the items on their lists and to put a smiley face next to each item they find.

To make it more interesting, let kids complete their lists by picking up the items, then have kids use them later to create nifty nature pictures. When you get to where you're going, let groups display their items. Spend time thanking God for all the wonderful things he gave us to enjoy!

hum that tune

Best For: Kindergarten through sixth grade
Energy Level: Low
Supplies: Small slips of paper, pencils, and a bag

THE GAME:

Have this game ready for your next trip, and your vehicle will be alive with the sound of music.

Write familiar song titles on small slips of paper and place them in a bag before this game. Have passengers form groups. You may want to group them according to where they are sitting: front, middle, and back seats. If you are traveling with a small group, have the children form pairs. Ask each person to choose one role to play in his or her group: hummer, clapper, or snapper. (When playing with pairs, use only hummers and clappers.)

Let each team pick a slip of paper from the bag and hum, clap, and snap the familiar tune while the other teams try to identify the song. Have the group that identifies the tune first pick a slip and hum, clap, and snap a different tune for everyone else to identify. For added fun, have all the passengers in the vehicle sing one round of each song together.

switch swap

Best For: Second through sixth grade
Energy Level: Medium
Supplies: Colored plastic beads, lunch sacks, and a watch
                    with a second hand

THE GAME:

This game is perfect to play while your group is hiking or walking during a retreat. It works best with four or more small groups.

Fill four lunch sacks (or more—one for each group) with a mixture of eight colored plastic beads. Invite kids to form small groups, and hand each group a sack. Have kids brainstorm in their small groups how they'll trade with other groups to collect eight beads of the same color. Tell kids they'll have only two minutes to trade and they must keep walking as they play. After two minutes, see how many groups were able to accomplish their "colorful" goal, then mix up the colors and have the kids play again.

If you use beads, save them and play Just Bead It! as a follow-up activity. You'll find this game on page 24.

song spotters

Best For: Kindergarten through third grade
Energy Level: Low
Supplies: None

THE GAME:

Incorporate sing-alongs into a trip.

Encourage children to look out the windows while you're traveling. Have them take turns calling out items they see along the road; for example, cows, houses, cars, grass, or people. When one child picks out something he or she notices, help kids think of a song that has that word in it. If a child picked "grass," suggest singing "And the Green Grass Grew All Around." Continue playing until everyone has picked an item. Let children try to think of songs on their own.

For a twist, encourage kids to make up their own songs, using familiar melodies. For example, sing, "I see mud all over the ground, over the ground, over the ground. I see mud all over the ground, right outside my window" to the tune of "The Mulberry Bush." Get your kids singing a new tune, and they'll be laughing all the way to your destination.

bible signs

Best For: All ages
Energy Level: Low
Supplies: Optional: a dictionary and a Bible

THE GAME:

When traveling in a car or bus, kids love to play The ABC Game, using street signs and billboards. Use this variation to reinforce a biblical lesson or topic and have fun at the same time.

Have kids check out road signs, billboards, and license plates to find the letters in certain words found in the Bible. For younger kids, use simple words like Bible, Jesus, God, pray, and love. Have older kids spell books of the Bible, names of prophets, or biblical places. Let kids use the Bible to look up words they may not know how to spell.

pass it on

Best For: Third through sixth grade
Energy Level: Low
Supplies: Pieces of paper, pencils, and small slips of paper

THE GAME:

This game will keep older kids quiet and busy for a long time.

Before the game, write each child's name on a small slip of paper.

Pass out a piece of paper and a pencil to each child. Ask kids to write their names at the top. Explain that everyone will work together to create stories. Each person will add one sentence to every paper. Hand out one of the slips of paper to each child. Make sure no one receives his or her own name on the slip of paper, and encourage kids to keep the names they receive secret.

Tell everyone to use that person's name in each sentence they write, but instruct the kids that the sentences must be upbeat and positive. Allow one minute of writing time for each paper.

When papers are returned to their owners, let kids take turns reading the stories out loud.

You'll have fun listening to the creative results of your traveling troupe!

bunches of scrunches

Best For: Kindergarten through second grade
Energy Level: Low
Supplies: None

THE GAME:

Make your walking trip fun and fast with this sensory game.

Name a sensory category such as squishy, crunchy, slippery, monstrous, itsy-bitsy, or shiny. Have kids call out items that fit in the category named. Give an example so the kids will know how to play. If your category is squishy, mention mud as a possible answer. Tell kids that they can say anything they think fits in the category. Answers may be limited to things the kids find while walking, or you may allow kids to think up new, creative ideas. To rule out litter or trash kids may encounter along the way, you may want to limit ideas to things God has created.

Here are some great sensory categories to get you started:

- **squishy**—mud, soggy pickles, wet cement;
- **crunchy**—potato chips, snow, peanuts, sticks, dry leaves;
- **slippery**—ice, banana peel, slimy moss, linoleum;
- **monstrous**—tall building, tree, power poles;
- **itsy-bitsy**—bugs, ants, seeds, leaves; and
- **shiny**—car chrome, windows, the sun.

bean traders

Best For: All ages
Energy Level: Medium
Supplies: A bag of mixed dried beans, plastic sandwich bags, and a bag of small candies

THE GAME:

Before playing, divide the mixed dried beans into plastic sandwich bags. Make sure there are no more than three of any one bean type and no more than 10 beans per bag.

Have kids form groups of three or four. Hand each child a bag of beans to trade within his or her group. Explain that the goal is to get as many sets as possible. A set consists of five beans of the same type.

Have kids switch groups after 15 seconds then continue trading. Allow four switches, then call time. Let kids count how many bean sets they formed. Play once more, then hand each child a "set" of small candies, such as candy corn, to munch.

pass the pillow

Best For: All ages
Energy Level: Low
Supplies: A small pillow

THE GAME:

This game may put a few kids to sleep on your trip, but they'll have sweet dreams.

You'll need a small pillow. Tell kids that it's a make-believe-dream pillow. Explain that as you pass the pillow, everyone is going to help create a dream. Have the first person begin by holding the pillow and saying, "I had a dream and..." then filling in the rest of the sentence with something serious or something kooky! As each child holds the pillow, have him or her add a few words to the dream.

Challenge kids to add descriptive words that creatively keep the dream going. See if you can make it around the whole group, then let someone start a new dream!

rhyme time

Best For: Kindergarten through second grade
Energy Level: Low
Supplies: Any Dr. Seuss book

THE GAME:

Kids will love playing this rhyming game. Keep a Dr. Seuss book nearby to help you think of new rhymes.

Have one child begin by counting, beginning with number one and saying a word of one or two syllables. Direct the child next to him to say the number two and a word that rhymes with the first word. The next child says the next number and does the same or passes if he or she can't think of a word. Here's an example: One-cat, two-sat, three-hat, four-mat, five-fat, six-gnat, seven-rat. If someone is having trouble thinking of a word, let him or her glance through the Dr. Seuss book for hints or helps. When everyone has passed, have the next child begin with number one and think of a word to start the game again. Challenge kids to reach 10 rhyming words.

For a variation, have kids clap every time they begin their turn and say a number.

shape surprises

Best For: Kindergarten through sixth grade
Energy Level: Low
Supplies: Sheets of paper and pencils

THE GAME:

Keep your group happy, quiet, and creative on your next road trip.
Pass out a sheet of paper and a pencil to each child. Instruct kids to draw shapes such as circles, squares, or triangles. Let kids decide which shapes they'll draw. Have kids write their names at the top of their papers. Then instruct everyone to pass the drawing to another person. Have that person add something to the picture, using one of the shapes, then pass the paper to another player. Have kids continue drawing and passing pictures until everyone has his or her original paper back. Play the game several times.

Challenge older children to write sentences telling something about their shapes. Have each child add a sentence to each paper as it is passed.

thought thinkers

Best For: Second through sixth grade
Energy Level: Low
Supplies: None

THE GAME:

Make sure your kids are wide-awake for this game, because it requires some thought!

Choose a child to be the first "thinker." Ask the child to think of an object without telling anyone else what it is. Then have the thinker ask each person in the group, "What is my thought like?" Let each child respond with one word without knowing what the thinker is thinking of. Children can respond by saying things like big, red, wet, old, or any other descriptive word. Once everyone has said what they think, let the thinker say what object he or she had in mind. Then have the thinker ask each child, "Why is (the object he or she thought of) (whatever that child said)?" For example, if the thinker had been thinking of a barn and the first child said "wet," he or she could respond, "A barn gets wet when it rains." Play continues until everyone has answered the thinker's second question and everyone has been a thinker.

This will keep minds alert and active without letting kids dwell on how far they have to travel.

- -

seeing eye dogs

Best For: First through third grade
Energy Level: Low
Supplies: None

THE GAME:

While taking a walking trip, form trios. Have one student in each trio close his or her eyes. The other two students will act as "Seeing Eye dogs," gently holding the child's arms to safely guide him or her. Encourage the Seeing Eye dogs to give to the "blind" child detailed descriptions of what they see, such as people, colors, clouds, flowers, and trees. If you're traveling a familiar route, see if the blind person can describe the view as he or she remembers it. After two minutes, have students switch roles. Have kids play until everyone has played each part.

Upon arriving at your destination, have kids recall one or two special things they "saw" through their Seeing Eye dogs.

- -

pastor's pet parrot

Best For: Second through sixth grade
Energy Level: Low
Supplies: None

THE GAME:

Have a terrific tongue-twisting time with this game!

Let kids play this funny alphabet game in pairs. Have one pair begin by saying, "The pastor's pet parrot is a(n) _____ pest!" Instruct the partners to fill in the blank with any descriptive word beginning with "a," such as "awesome" or "ancient." Have the next pair repeat the sentence, changing the first pair's word to a "b" word such as "brown" or "bumpy." Have kids play until they've gone through the whole alphabet—or until everyone's tongue is too twisted to talk!

For a fun variation, let kids come up with their own funny phrases.

chasing cheetahs in chile

Best For: Second through sixth grade
Energy Level: Low
Supplies: None

THE GAME:

This letter game has a fun twist that will bring out the giggles in any group.

Let kids form pairs. Have one pair begin by asking partners sitting beside them, "Where are you going?" That pair names a place such as "Cincinnati" or "the moon." Then have the first pair ask, "What will you do there?" Instruct the partners to respond with two words starting with the same letter as the place to which they said they are traveling. A sample dialogue might go something like this:

child one: "Where are you going?"
child two: "To Florida."
child one: "What will you do there?"
child two: "Flip flapjacks."

Then have the children who answered the questions ask the next "Where are you going?" Continue playing until everyone has had a turn to ask and answer the questions.

To add a little more tongue-twisting terror, try three-word responses.

big cat, little cat

Best For: Kindergarten through second grade
Energy Level: Low
Supplies: None

THE GAME:

This game is especially fun for the young children in your group.

Choose one child to be the "big cat." The rest of the kids will be "little cats." Have the big cat close his or her eyes. Explain that each time the big cat meows, you'll point to a little cat who must answer with a "mew." Then the big cat will have three tries to guess who mewed. If the big cat guesses successfully, he or she may choose the next big cat. If the big cat can't guess which little cat mewed, he or she must remain the big cat for another turn. Have kids keep playing until everyone has had a chance to be the big cat.

For a variation, try letting two or three little cats mew at the same time. This may drive the driver crazy, but it's a lot of fun on the road!

this way, that way

Best For: All ages
Energy Level: Low
Supplies: Paper and pencils

THE GAME:

Invite your group to think of a few well-known fairy tales such as "Little Red Hen," "Three Bears," and "Gingerbread Man." Make a list of the fairy tales. Announce the first story from the list. For example, it might be "Cinderella." Ask one child to begin telling the story. Explain that he or she will tell the first part of the tale, using something that is visible from his or her window. For example, a child may see a barn outside the window and say, "Once upon a time there was a girl called Cinderella. She lived in a *barn* and had to work all the time for her mean stepsisters." The next child continues the story.

Challenge kids to recall each other's items and to keep them in the story. Have kids continue until everyone has had a turn to add to the story. Refer to your fairy tale list if you want to start a new story.

Mumbo Jumbo

Best For: All ages
Energy Level: Low
Supplies: One stuffed animal

THE GAME:

Everyone loves stuffed animals. In this game the animal helps kids remember each other's names. Play this game if you're traveling with a group that needs to get acquainted.

Before the game, find a stuffed animal and pick out a crazy name for it, such as Jumbo. Hold up the animal so everyone can see it, and introduce the stuffed animal to the group. Then hand the animal to the person closest to you and say, "My name is Fred (or whatever your name is), and this is Jumbo." Have the next player take the animal and pass it to the closest person and say, "My name is (name), and Fred says this is Jumbo." Tell kids they'll have to listen closely to each other's names to remember them. Let the animal travel around the group. If kids can't remember someone's name, let others give clues.

After you're done playing, everyone will know each other and you'll have a great mascot for the rest of the trip!

everyone's-a-winner games for children's ministry

energy-level index

high-energy games

medium-energy games

low-eNergy games